To my nieces, nephews and godchildren – all fifteen of you.
May you learn that praying can be fun – J.B.

For my family – Dad, Mum, Tania, Steven and Lisa-Marie,
and friends – Katie, Sharon, Alison, Sophie, Bertrand and Frances McKay – E.G.

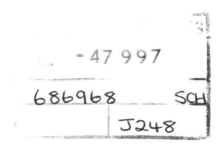

A World of Prayers copyright © Frances Lincoln Limited 2005
Text copyright © Jeremy Brooks 2005
Illustrations copyright © Elena Gomez 2005

First published in Great Britain in 2005 by Frances Lincoln Children's Books,
4 Torriano Mews, Torriano Avenue, London NW5 2RZ
www.franceslincoln.com

Prayer for the peoples of the Middle East from *Morning, Noon and Night*, ed. John Carden,
Church Mission Society (London, 1979), page 83, ISBN 900287 26 8
The publishers apologise to any copyright holders they were unable to trace
and would like to hear from them.

British Library Cataloguing in Publication Data available on request

ISBN 1-84507-087-9
Set in Bembo

Printed in Singapore
1 3 5 7 9 8 6 4 2

A World of
Prayers

Selected by the Revd Jeremy Brooks

Illustrated by Elena Gomez

FRANCES LINCOLN CHILDREN'S BOOKS

Introduction

Grown-ups often find it difficult to pray. They think a solemn voice is needed and special words should be said. But an amazing thing about prayer is that children all around the world have been praying for hundreds of years and often they do not have the same difficulty that adults do!

Some of the prayers in this book may make you laugh, but I don't think God will mind. Some need to be spoken out aloud and enjoyed as a rhyme; some can be said quietly to yourself and will make you think.

Some prayers are said by children all over the world in many different languages. Here is one version of the Lord's Prayer that we say in English and, next to it, how it looks in Chinese. You'd never guess they were the same prayer!

Our Father in heaven,
Hallowed be your name,
Your kingdom come, your will be done
On earth as in heaven.
Give us today our daily bread.
Forgive us our sins
As we forgive those who sin against us.
Lead us not into temptation,
But deliver us from evil.
For the kingdom, the power
and the glory are yours,
Now and for ever,
AMEN

我们在天上的父，
愿人都尊你的名为圣。
愿你的国将临，
愿你的旨意行在地上，
如同行在天上。
我们日用的饮食。
免我们的债，
如同我们免了人的债。
不叫我们遇见试探；
救我们脱离凶恶。
因为国度，权柄，荣耀，
全是你的，直到永远。
阿门。

Sometimes we can pray as we rush along, and some of the prayers in the book can be said in a hurry. But sometimes we need to stop and be quiet and say the prayers quietly. Children in the Philippines sometimes sing this little prayer before they say their other prayers, to help them to be quiet.

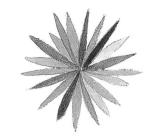

We'll bow our heads,
We'll close our eyes
Before we start to pray.
We'll think of Jesus listening,
And mean the words we say.

I hope that these prayers will help you to pray in the morning, at night, at mealtimes, and to ask God to give others good things. You don't need to use other people's words to pray — often it is better to use your own — but maybe some of these will help you to find your own special words.

Prayers for the Morning

In some parts of the world, there are prayers for different things people do and for different times of the day. We are used to prayers for mealtimes, but in other places there might also be prayers for planting seeds in the fields, for going fishing, for working in the kitchen – every activity would be covered by a prayer. The prayers that I have chosen can be used in the morning, as you think about all the things you will do during the day.

I go forth today
In the might of heaven,
In the brightness of the sun,
In the whiteness of snow,
In the splendour of fire,
In the speed of lightning,
In the swiftness of wind,
In the firmness of rock.
I go forth today
In the hand of God.

Ireland

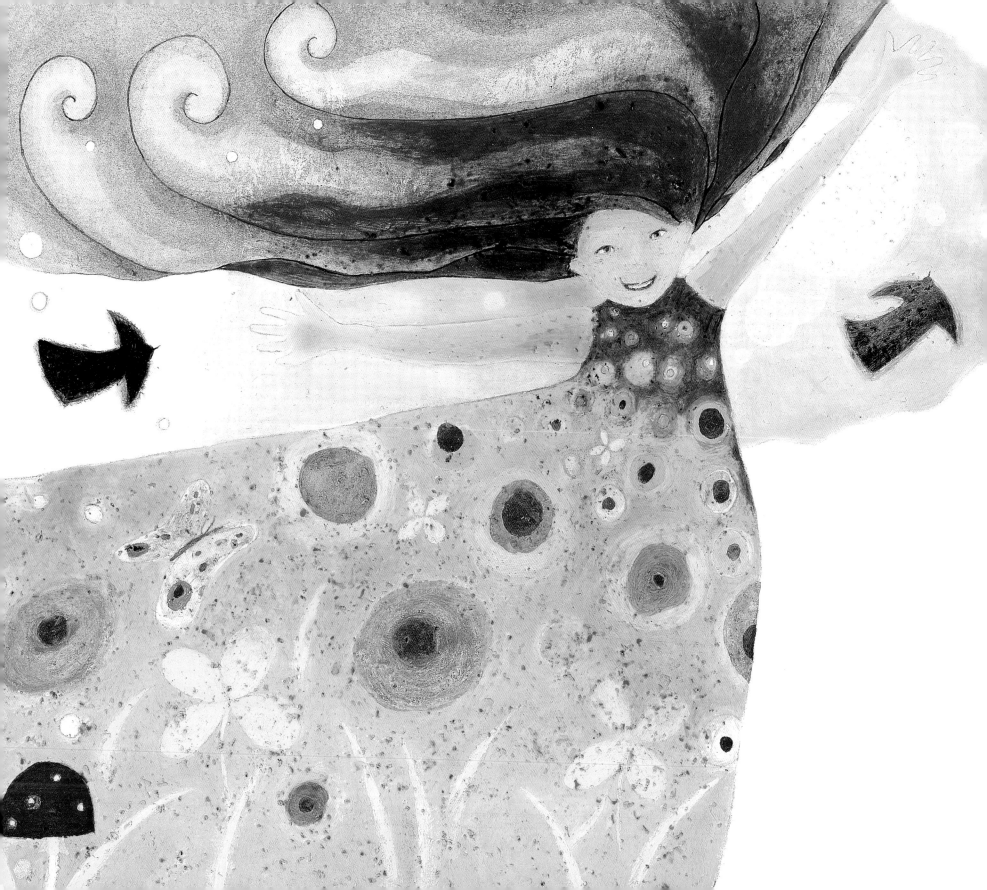

Enjoy the earth gently,
Enjoy the earth gently,
For if the earth is spoiled
It cannot be repaired.
Enjoy the earth gently.

Yoruba prayer, Ivory Coast

Give me the strength to meet
    each day with quiet will.
Give me the faith to know
    you are my shepherd still.
Give me the light to find
    my way when shadows fall,
Be my steady guiding star,
    Father of all.

Israel

Dear God,
Be good to me today.
The sea is so wide
And my boat is so small.

Breton Fishermen, France

May my mouth praise the love of God this morning.

O God, may I do your will this day.

May my ears hear the words of God and obey them.

O God, may I do your will this day.

May my feet follow the footsteps of God this day.

O God, may I do your will this day.

Japan

O God,
Help me never to judge another
Until I have walked two weeks in his moccasins.

Native American, Sioux

O God, you know how busy I must be this day.
If I forget you, please don't forget me.

England

Mealtime Graces

One of the most important things we do when we pray is to say "thank you". And one of the things that we can remember to say thank you for is our food. We can do this three times a day. See if you can pick out your favourite breakfast, lunch and supper grace.

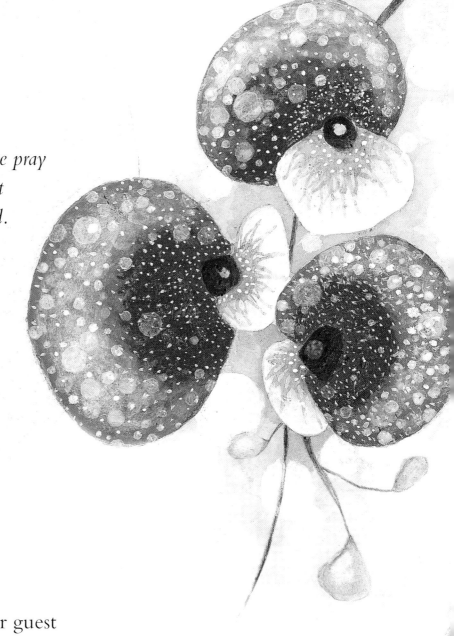

Come, Lord Jesus, be our guest
And let these gifts to us be blessed.

Germany

Each time we eat,
    May we remember God's love.

China

Give us Lord, a bit o' sun,
A bit o' work and a bit o' fun.
Give us all in the struggle and sputter
Our daily bread and a bit o' butter.

England

O You who feed the little bird,
Bless our food, O Lord.

Norway

Doon head,
Up paws,
Thank God
We've jaws.

Scotland

The bread is warm and fresh,
The water cool and clear.
Lord of all life, be with us,
Lord of all life, be near.

Nigeria

The eagles give thanks for the mountains,
The fish give thanks for the sea,
We give thanks for our blessings
And for what we're about to receive.

Native American

Prayers for Night-time

Just as people have always said prayers
for what they do during the day, so they also
pray at night before they go to sleep.
Here is a selection of prayers to be used at bedtime.

Dear Jesus,
As a hen covers her chicks
With her wings to keep them safe,
Protect us this dark night
Under your golden wings.

India

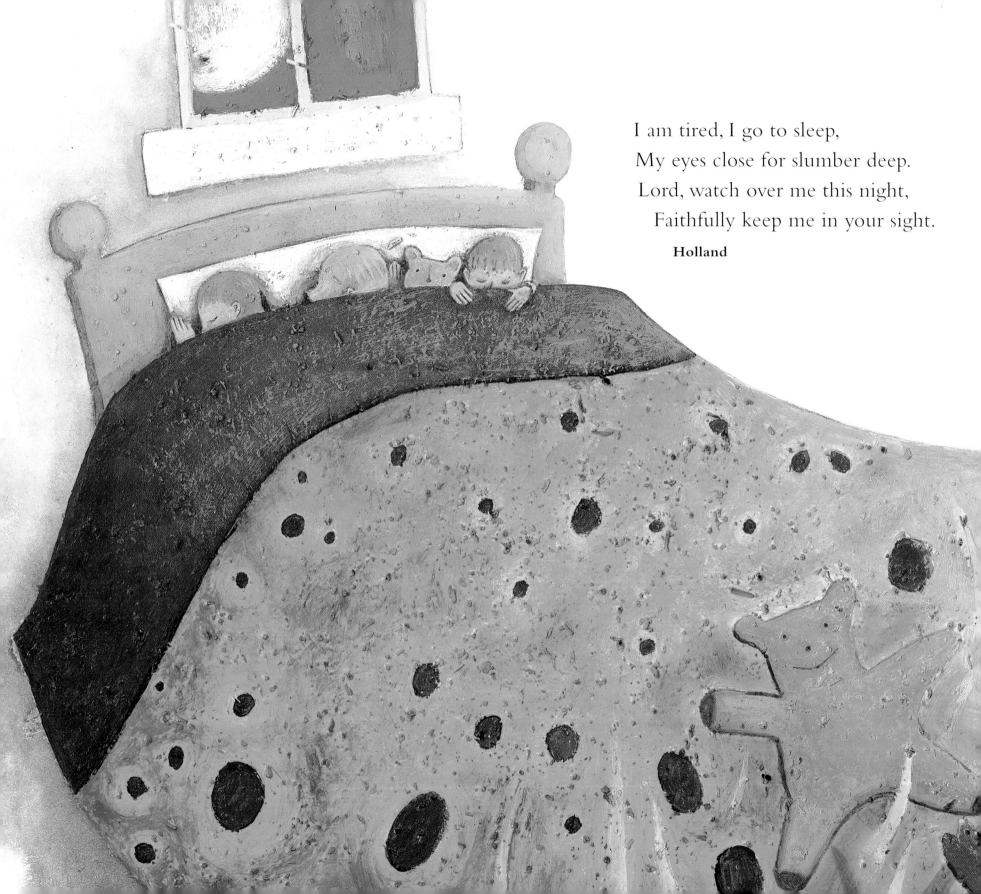

I am tired, I go to sleep,
My eyes close for slumber deep.
Lord, watch over me this night,
Faithfully keep me in your sight.

Holland

Silence through the lands tonight,
Sleep and fold our hands tonight.
God will watch us till the morning,
Through the night till day is dawning.
Safe from danger, free from warning
Are we tonight.

Holland

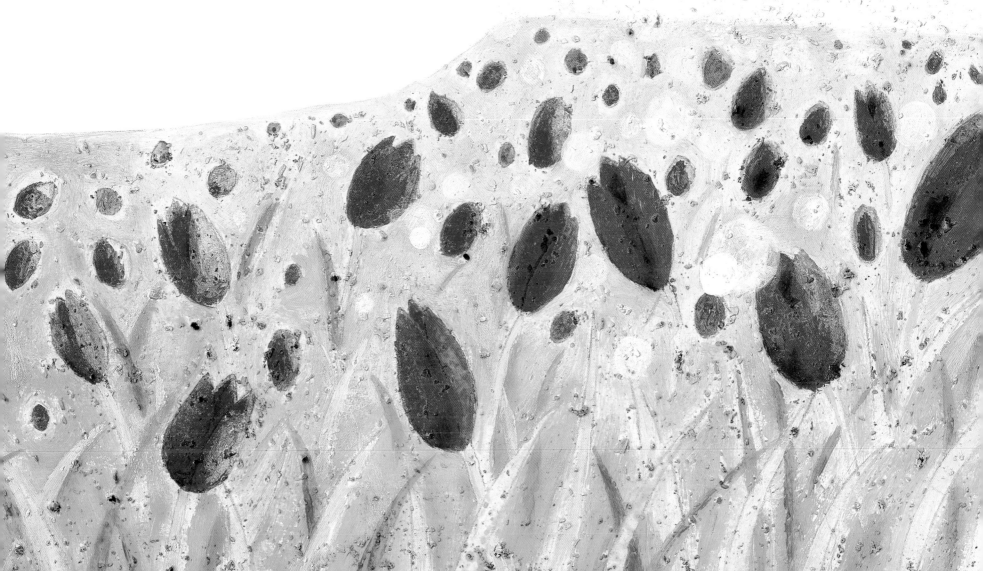

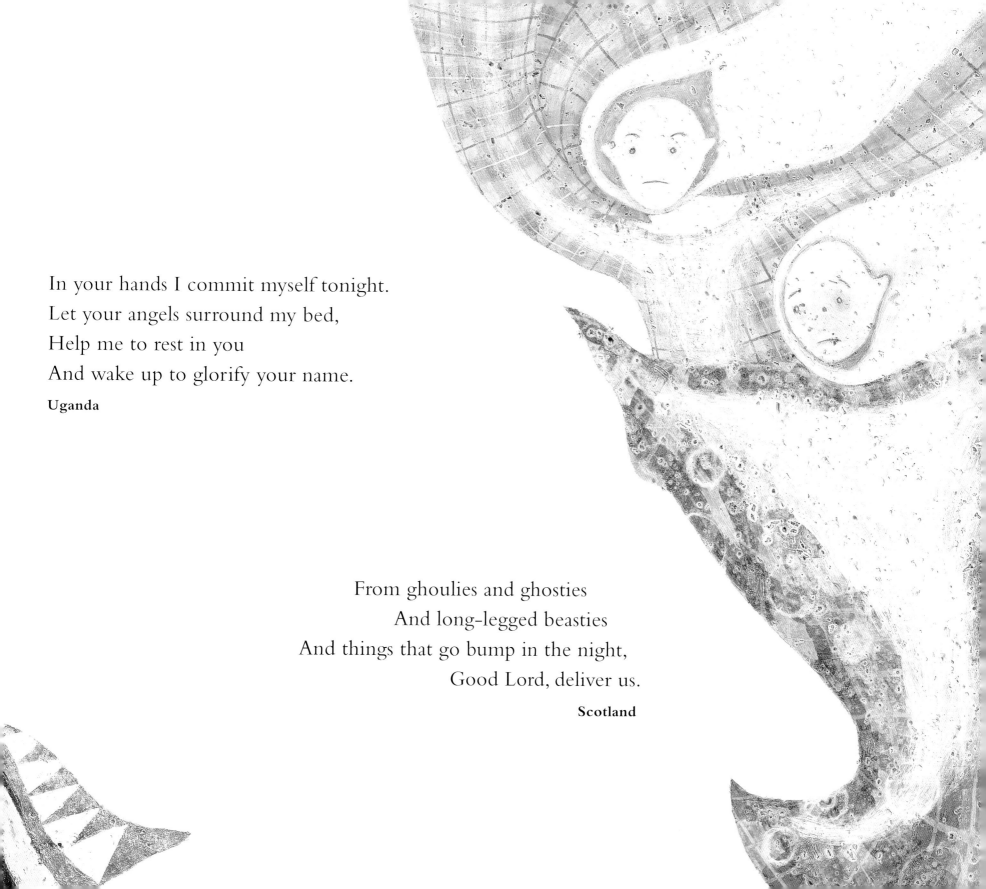

In your hands I commit myself tonight.
Let your angels surround my bed,
Help me to rest in you
And wake up to glorify your name.

Uganda

From ghoulies and ghosties
And long-legged beasties
And things that go bump in the night,
Good Lord, deliver us.

Scotland

O make my heart so still, so still,
When I am deep in prayer,
That I might hear the white mist-wreaths
Losing themselves in air!

Japan

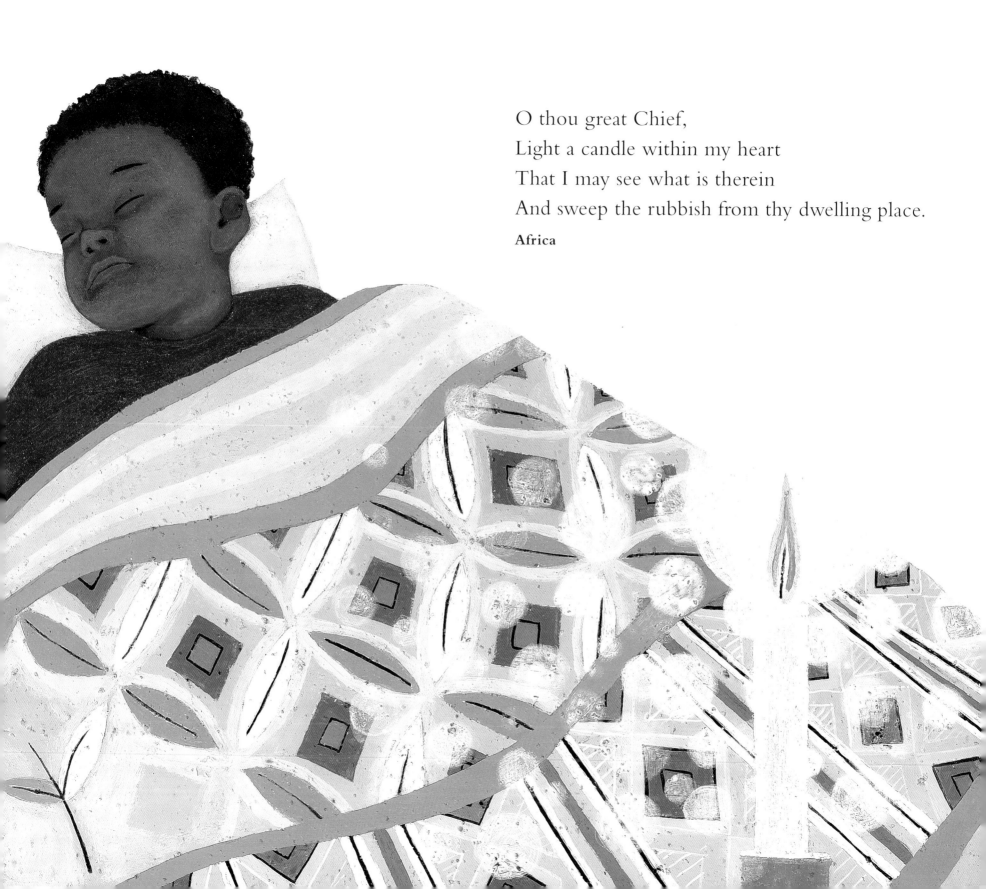

O thou great Chief,
Light a candle within my heart
That I may see what is therein
And sweep the rubbish from thy dwelling place.

Africa

Blessings

*Blessings are one of the oldest forms of prayers.
They are prayers for other people, wishing that God
would look after them and give them good things.
Countries have different ideas of what is good —
in Kenya, it is a blessing to be told that you are
like a cloud that always brings rain, but it would not
be such a blessing in Great Britain!*

May God raise you up above everything,
Spread out like water of a lake.
Be abundance that never ends,
That never changes.
Be like a mountain,
Be like a camel,
Be like a cloud – a cloud that brings rain always.

Samburu prayer, Kenya

O Lord Jesus,
Stretch forth thy wounded hands
In blessing over thy people,
To heal and to restore,
And to draw them to thyself
And to one another in love.

Middle East

God bless all those that I love,
God bless all those that love me,
God bless all those that love those that I love,
And all those that love those that love me.

New England, USA

God's love for us all
Is really wonderful.
God's love for us all
Is really wonderful.
It reaches up to the skies
And down to the seas,
It goes way out in front of us
And follows on behind.
It spreads out through the land
　　to all the world.

God's blessing for us all
Is really wonderful,
God's blessing for us all
Is really wonderful.
It reaches up to the skies,
And down to the seas,
It goes way out in front of us
And follows on behind.
It spreads out through the land
　　to all the world.

East Africa

Peace of the running waves to you,
Deep peace of the flowing air to you,
Deep peace of the quiet earth to you,
Deep peace of the shining stars to you,
Deep peace of the shades of night to you,
Moon and stars always giving light to you,
Deep peace of Christ, the Son of Peace, to you.

Scotland